**W9-CNR-925**

Manta Rays

Judy Wearing

Published by Weigl Publishers Inc.
350 5th Avenue, 59th Floor
New York, NY 10118
Website: www.weigl.com

Library of Congress Cataloging-in-Publication Data available upon request.
Fax 1-866-44-WEIGL for the attention of the Publishing Records department.

ISBN 978-1-60596-104-0 (hard cover)
ISBN 978-1-60596-105-7 (soft cover)

Printed in the United States of America in North Mankato, Minnesota
3 4 5 6 7 8 9 0 14 13 12 11 10

112010
WEP281110

Editor: Heather C. Hudak
Design and Layout: Terry Paulhus

All of the Internet URLs given in the book were valid at the time of publication. However, due to the dynamic nature of
the Internet, some addresses may have changed, or sites may have ceased to exist since publication. While the author
and publisher regret any inconvenience this may cause readers, no responsibility for any such changes can be accepted
by either the author or the publisher.

Every reasonable effort has been made to trace ownership and to obtain permission to reprint copyright material. The
publishers would be pleased to have any errors or omissions brought to their attention so that they may be corrected
in subsequent printings.

Weigl acknowledges Getty Images as its primary image supplier for this title.

CONTENTS

What is a Manta Ray?

Have you ever seen a fish that looks like a flying pancake? This may have been a manta ray.

Manta rays have very flat, wide bodies. The **fins** on their sides look like wings. This gives them a diamond shape.

Manta means "blanket" in Spanish. Why do you think this fish is named after a blanket?

Family Ties

Did you know that manta rays are **related** to sharks and stingrays? Sharks are known for their big teeth. Stingrays have a **stinger** on their tail.

Manta rays are different from these fish. They do not have big teeth or a stinger. Most manta rays lay flat on the sea floor, hidden in the sand. They swim smoothly and slowly in open water.

Gentle Giants

Can you imagine a baby the size of a bathtub? This is the size of a baby manta ray. Baby manta rays are about 5 feet (1.5 meters) wide at birth.

Manta rays are huge animals. Adults are more than 22 feet (6.7 m) wide. This is the size of a small plane. The largest manta ray ever seen was 30 feet (9 m) long.

Color Coded

Have you ever had your fingerprints taken? No one else has the same prints as you. In this same way, each manta ray has its own pattern of colors.

On top, manta rays are black, gray, or blue. This helps them blend in with the water. Manta rays are white or gray on the bottom. Looking up from under a manta ray, it will blend in with the sky above.

Keeping Clean

How do manta rays keep their skin clean and germ free? Special cleaner fish help them do this.

Cleaner fish wait for manta rays in **coral reefs**. Manta rays stay at the reef while these fish eat small animals and germs off their skin.

Manta rays have a thick layer of **slime** on their skin to protect it from germs.

What a Big Mouth

How do manta rays eat their food? They have two long lumps on their head. These are used like spoons to scoop water and food into their mouth.

A manta ray swims with its mouth open. Water flows into the mouth and out through **gills** at the bottom of the body. Food is trapped at the back of the mouth.

Manta rays eat small plants and animals called plankton that float in the ocean.

15

Living Alone

How would you feel if you lived alone? Manta rays prefer to live alone. They only gather together once each year.

Manta rays gather in groups between December and April to **mate**. More than one year later, a baby manta ray is born with its fins curled up. The baby soon stretches out and swims away.

In the Air

Have you ever seen a fish jump into the air? Some manta rays can jump right out of the water. They may even do this two or three times in a row.

Some scientists think manta rays are playing when they jump out of the water. Others believe this helps remove germs from their skin.

The sound of a manta ray splashing down can be heard for miles (kilometers).

Friendly Fish

Would you like to see a manta ray in nature? Many manta rays are curious about humans.

Manta rays may come near people who are swimming in the ocean. They often swim beside divers. People should keep a safe distance from manta rays. Touching one may remove the slime from its skin. This can make the manta ray sick.

Eat Like a Manta

Supplies
two small plastic bags, a large tray filled with water, scissors, and 10 to 20 sunflower seeds in the shell

1. Put the seeds in the water. This is plankton floating in the ocean.

2. Hold a plastic bag open, and move it around in the tray of water. This is like a manta ray swimming through the ocean. Can you catch the plankton? Pull the bag out of the water. Put the sunflower seeds that you caught back in the water.

3. With the scissors, cut five slits in the bottom of the other plastic bag. These are the gills of a manta ray. The gills should be about 1 inch (2.5 centimeters) apart.

4. Now, move the bag with the slits through the water. Is it easier or harder to catch the seeds? How do gills help manta rays eat plankton?

Find Out More

To learn more about manta rays, visit these websites.

Stanford University
www.stanford.edu/group/
microdocs/mantaray.html

Georgia Aquarium
www.georgiaaquarium.org/
nandi/about-nandi

**San Diego Natural
History Museum**
www.oceanoasis.org/
fieldguide/mant-bir.html

The Manta Network
www.mantas.org

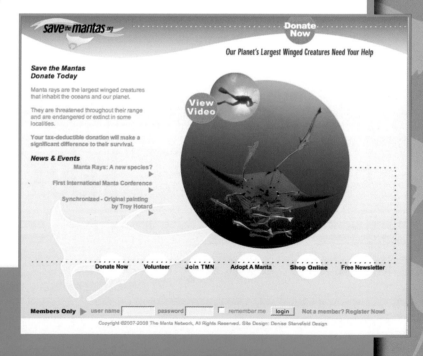

Glossary

coral reefs: large, stony structures that are made by a soft animal in the ocean; many plants and animals live on reefs

fins: flat flaps that stick out from the body of an animal that lives in water; used for swimming

gills: organs that are used by animals that live in water to breathe

mate: when a male and female come together to have young

related: to belong to the same family

slime: a thick, slippery substance

stinger: a sharp, pointed part of an animal that pierces the skin and causes pain

Index